Mark McGwire

...he words of

...ussa

...Brock

...an Musial

Willie McG...

Greg Mad...

Bob Costa...

Copy... 1998 by Dr. James Beckett
All ri... reserved under International
and ...an-American Copyright
Conventions.

Published by: Beckett Pub...
15850 Dallas Parkway
Dallas, TX 75248
ISBN: 1-887432-63-9

Second Edition: December 1998
...Corporate S...es and
...72) ...-6657

70!

No.	Date	Opposing Team / Pitcher	Distance
1	3/31	L.A. / Ramon Martinez	364
2	4/2	L.A. / Frank Lankford	368
3	4/3	S.D. / Mark Langston	364
4	4/4	S.D. / Don Wengert	419
5	4/14	ARIZ / Jeff Suppan	424
6	4/14	ARIZ / Jeff Suppan	347
7	4/14	ARIZ / Barry Manuel	462
8	4/17	PHIL / Matt Whiteside	419
9	4/21	at MON / Trey Moore	437
10	4/25	at PHIL / Jerry Spradlin	419
11	4/30	at CHI (NL) / Marc Pisciotta	371
12	5/1	at CHI (NL) / Rod Beck	362
13	5/8	at N.Y. (NL) / Rick Reed	358
14	5/12	MIL / Paul Wagner	527
15	5/14	ATL / Kevin Millwood	381
16	5/16	FLA / Livan Hernandez	545
17	5/18	FLA / Jesus Sanchez	478
18	5/19	at PHIL / Tyler Green	440
19	5/19	at PHIL / Tyler Green	471
20	5/19	at PHIL / Wayne Gomes	451
21	5/22	S.F. / Mark Gardner	425
22	5/23	S.F. / Rich Rodriguez	366
23	5/23	S.F. / John Johnstone	477
24	5/24	S.F / Robb Nen	397
25	5/25	COL / John Thomson	433
26	5/29	at S.D. / Dan Miceli	388
27	5/30	at S.D. / Andy Ashby	423
28	6/5	S.F. / Orel Hershiser	409
29	6/8	at CHI (AL) / Jason Bere	356
30	6/10	at CHI (AL) / Jim Parque	409
31	6/12	at ARIZ / Andy Benes	438
32	6/17	at HOU / Jose Lima	437
33	6/18	at HOU / Shane Reynolds	449
34	6/24	at CLE / Jaret Wright	433
35	6/25	at CLE / Dave Burba	461
36	6/27	at MIN / Mike Trombley	431
37	6/30	K.C. / Glendon Rusch	472
38	7/11	HOU / Billy Wagner	485
39	7/12	HOU / Sean Bergman	405
40	7/12	HOU / Scott Elarton	415
41	7/17	L.A. / Brian Bohannon	511
42	7/17	L.A. / Antonio Osuna	425
43	7/20	at S.D. / Brian Boehringer	458
44	7/26	at COL / John Thomson	452
45	7/28	MIL / Mike Myers	408
46	8/8	CHI (NL) / Mark Clark	354
47	8/11	N.Y. (NL) / Bobby Jones	464
48	8/19	CHI (NL) / Matt Karchner	398
49	8/19	CHI (NL) / Terry Mulholland	409
50	8/20	N.Y. (NL) / Willie Blair	369
51	8/20	N.Y. (NL) / Rick Reed	385
52	8/22	PITT / Francisco Cordova	477
53	8/23	PITT / Ricardo Rincon	393
54	8/26	FLA / Justin Speier	509
55	8/30	ATL / Dennis Martinez	501
56	9/1	FLA / Livan Hernandez	450
57	9/1	FLA / Donn Pall	472
58	9/2	FLA / Brian Edmondson	497
59	9/2	FLA / Rob Stanifer	458
60	9/5	CIN / Dennis Reyes	381
61	9/7	CHI (NL) / Mike Morgan	430
62	9/8	CHI (NL) / Steve Trachsel	341
63	9/15	PITT / Jason Christiansen	385
64	9/18	MIL / Rafael Roque	341
65	9/20	MIL / Scott Karl	423
66	9/25	MON / Shayne Bennett	375
67	9/26	MON / Dustin Hermanson	403
68	9/26	MON / Kirk Bullinger	435
69	9/27	MON / Mike Thurman	377
70	9/27	MON / Carl Pavano	370

Where were you for 62?

On that magical night of Sept. 8, I was lucky enough to be right behind home plate, midway up in Busch Stadium, in the first row of the press box with my colleagues from the St. Louis Post-Dispatch.

With one monumental shot, McGwire did more than just pass Roger Maris, whose 61 homers in a season stood as the big-league record for 37 years. Big Mac's home run No. 62 sent ripple after wonderful ripple through this nation. And not just through the relatively small corner occupied by sports.

McGwire, of the St. Louis Cardinals, and Sammy Sosa of the Chicago Cubs did more than make folks forget for awhile about this troubled world. They stood for the bedrock values that supported this country through other shaky times.

Both sluggers faced constant scrutiny, yet they reacted with class and courtesy. They respected each other, as well as their fans and the game that made them rich. And nobody seemed to be grumping about millionaire ballplayers when Big Mac and Slammin' Sammy dueled into late summer for the preeminent record in sports.

Countless onlookers were smitten by the message. We present a special lineup of some of them here, each taking a break from their everyday business to give their unique perspective on Big Mac — not solely on his historic 1998 season,

but on his career and his development into the greatest slugger of his time.

Manager Tony La Russa was interviewed while he was alone in his Busch Stadium office watching a golf tournament before a game with Atlanta. Dave McKay, the unsung Cardinals coach and batting practice pitcher, spoke while sitting on an equipment trunk down the hallway. Stan Musial plopped down in the chair of traveling secretary C.J. Chere, then motioned me to take trainer Barry Weinberg's chair for our impromptu chat. Greg Maddux of Atlanta, the best pitcher of this generation, detailed his respect

for McGwire from the couch of the visitor's clubhouse at Busch.

And the list goes on. Buddy Bates, the modest Cardinals equipment manager, bustling around his memorabilia-cluttered office. Lou Brock, the Cardinals' Hall of Famer, stopping with his wife en route to a pregame ceremony to analyze Mark's appeal. Billy Williams, the Cubs' coach and perennial batting champ, talking hitting from the dugout at Three Rivers Stadium in Pittsburgh, on a weekend when Sosa launched Nos. 57 and 58. Willie McGee, on that same equipment trunk as McKay, forgetting his public stoicism to talk about his big teammate just before No. 62 left the premises.

Tim Forneris, the refreshing young groundskeeper who retrieved what was billed as a million-dollar ball, was interviewed in the bullpen near the spot he grabbed No. 62. Country singer Wynonna Judd, his fellow guest on "The David Letterman Show," later cooed, "There are still nice boys left in the world."

And Bob Costas, the conscience of baseball, with his feet up in his St. Louis office, outlining the big picture for Big Mac. Despite saturation coverage and the heat of the September chase, our lineup happily took time to fill you in on the Big Redhaired Machine.

That cooperation itself shows their admiration for the man. They take us onto the field, into the dugout and inside the locker room. Thanks to them, we can understand how Big Mac came to stage what one rival admirer called "the greatest show on earth."

And who knows? Maybe Big Mac and the rest of us can all get together and do it again sometime.

Tom Wheatley has covered the St. Louis Cardinals for 14 years while writing sports columns and features for the St. Louis Post-Dispatch. He lives in St. Louis with wife Suzanne, daughters Katie and Carrie and son Tommy.

Contents

Chapter 1

By Tony La Russa, manager of the St. Louis Cardinals

As told to Ann Wheatley

'He has developed into as great a power hitter as we've ever seen.'

The first time I saw Mark McGwire was when we brought him up in September 1986. I got the job as manager in the middle of the summer, and in September call-ups he came up. I think at first he made a bunch of outs. He might have hit a homer or two, and you could see he had an exciting looking swing. It was just as compact as it is now.

It's a full swing, but you don't think he's muscling the ball. He's sort of changed it over the years. He's improved it. He gets a little better extension now. He finishes it better. He'll center balls a little more often so he gets underspin, so when the ball gets in the air, it carries. When he came to spring training in 1987, we had to decide if we were going to make him into a third baseman or a first baseman. He had a really good arm.

We had a young prospect named Robbie Nelson at first. At that time, Carney Lansford was the third baseman, and we didn't know how long he was going to keep playing. It turned out he played a long time. When we went to spring training, we thought Mark was

He just wanted — and I mean literally — to see it and hit it, which is actually a smart approach for a young hitter. You can get overwhelmed with philosophy and mechanics when you're that inexperienced. To a kid, maybe if you just see that little white thing and swing, you've got a chance.

But we did worry as he got older that he would never want to get into the intricacies of how you have to adjust. Pitchers are always adjusting to him. And that's been a dramatic improvement. I mean, he is really a smart hitter. He makes terrific adjustments from game to game, and sometimes within the at-bat. He studies what he does. He thinks about it. When he was young, I knew he didn't want to complicate hitting.

The general rule is if you give a hitter a thousand at-bats, then a lot of the stuff he hears when he gets into pro ball starts to make sense. Things like: You get a sinkerball pitcher up. You get a high pitcher down. You can't cover both sides of the plate, so take one side or the other. Don't swing at a guy's out pitch. Take away the guy's best pitch.

When you're a young guy, it's like, "What the heck does all that mean?" But it all starts to make sense after you've been up a thousand times — if you're good enough to get a thousand at-bats in the big leagues. Now, Mark knows his swing better than anybody. He watches tapes of himself. He can look and see what his keys are.

And after so many years in the American League, now he's in the National League. I always think there's potential for a guy to struggle when he changes leagues, especially a hitter. I don't care how much tape you watch or what scouting reports you get, until you see a guy's fastball and see what his off-speed pitches are and see how he finishes out, you lose an edge. So I just think it's really impressive that he could hit 24 home runs in 51 games when he got here a year ago. And he spotted everybody eight games before he hit one. I think that's a real example of his talent. You've got to be pretty good to be able to do that. And it's an example of how strong he is mentally. That's why I knew he'd be fine near the end of his run at 61 homers. He won't give in to anything. The only question would be, does he get enough swings in the strike zone?

Mark was always a great guy who bought the team concept. He knew the reason we were all here was so our team could beat the other team — and, oh, by the way, if you have certain stats, you try to take those stats and make some money off them. It's not like the team is here to help you generate your stats and, oh, by the way, did we win?

Another important part of his development came when he first came up to the majors, and there was a core of strong, veteran team leaders in Oakland. To that extent, he was fortunate because he really learned a lot of major league lessons from first-class people. People like Carney and Dave Stewart and Dennis Eckersley and Ron Hassey and Dave Parker. And

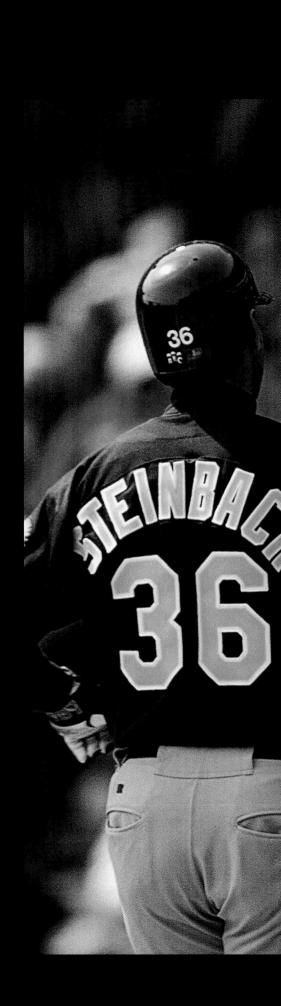

Mark would always prefer not talking about himself. And you see it now, when people are trying to talk to him about him. Back then, it was easier to blend into the background and let people talk to Jose Canseco or Rickey Henderson.

But what happened is the club started changing faces, and he started being a senior member of the club. I think we were all really impressed with how he took charge as the team leader. He and Terry Steinbach assumed the roles Carney Lansford and those other guys once held. Just like you weren't sure if he was going to spend a lot of time making adjustments at the plate, you weren't sure he'd ever jump up in the middle of the clubhouse and say, "Fellas, we need to go through that left door instead of the right one." But he developed into an outstanding spokesman.

And he still does that here in St. Louis. Well, there are times when he still doesn't feel that way about being vocal. But he's very vocal about what professionalism is. I mean, when you give a million dollars away every year (to charity) like Mark does . . . nobody else can do much better than that.

The bottom line with Mark is the complete package of what he developed into. When I say the whole package, I mean everything. He's smart about his nutrition. He's actually trimmed down so he's stronger and quicker.

And the discipline: He trains 30 minutes after a game. He's smart. He's dealing with pitchers now. He knows the mechanics of his swing. His swing is actually more consistent and better now than it was 10 years ago. He's a real good baserunner. And he's won a Gold Glove at first base.

He's got that great natural talent, but it includes something else. He has developed into — and history may show this — as great a power hitter as we've ever seen.

Tony La Russa managed in the American League for 17 years, including nine seasons with McGwire in Oakland, before he was hired by the Cardinals in 1995. He was named AL Manager of the Year three times and won one World Series, with the McGwire-led A's in 1989.

In 1998, McGwire became the first player ever to hit 50 home runs or more in three straight seasons.

Chapter 2

"I also don't have a problem walking him. If he wasn't so good, he might get better pitches to hit, don't you think?"

I've never really had the chance to get to know Mark McGwire. The first time we ever even ran into each other was at the All-Star Game this year, in the clubhouse in Denver. I pitched to him last year when he first came to the Cardinals. I have a lot of respect for him because of the type of hitter he is, but I pitch to him like I would any other power hitter.

You have to respect his power. I mean, he's a very good power hitter. He's probably the best to come along in awhile.

You have to respect his ability to hit an assortment of pitches over the fence. I knew he was big, but the guy's a really good hitter. It's fun to face him. As a pitcher, it's a great challenge. There are a lot of guys with good power nowadays. Sammy Sosa. Vinny Castilla. Andres Galarraga. Gary Sheffield. Barry Bonds. Greg Vaughn. Mike Piazza.

I think Mark's so popular with opposing players because he's respectful of the game. He's respectful of the guys he's playing with and the guys he plays against. I don't like it when I give up a home run. It ticks me off, and then sometimes I have to watch a guy dance around the bases yelling, "Yippie-ky-oh-ky-ay! Yee-haw! Look at me! Look at what I did!" and all that stuff. Then it can get to where you don't like that guy personally.

Now, I understand the hitters have a job to do. It's their job to try to hit the ball hard. I understand that. But it's not their job to do all that other stuff. As a pitcher, we're not doing cheerleader jumps when we strike a guy out for the second or third time in the game. And Mark doesn't do that when he hits a home run. He hits the ball out of the

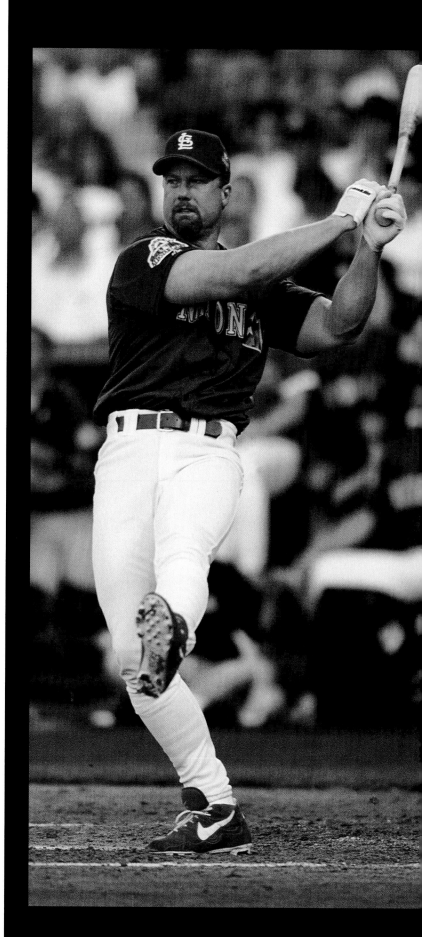

you sign it. That's protocol. But some guys just won't sign it.

Mark's real friendly. I've been on first base when he was playing there. He tries to talk to you, but I don't say anything back. I don't like to talk to those guys. They're hitters. I keep my distance. I say "Hi" or whatever, then hopefully I run to second, and then to third.

He is very good at first base. He's like Galarraga, another big guy who's good there defensively. McGwire's so good offensively that you forget about him defensively. He wants to be a complete player. You can tell that. If you have somebody who is good offensively and is also willing to play defense, that tells you something about a guy. The way McGwire hits the ball, he doesn't have to play defense. He only plays defense because he wants to.

He has pride in himself. If my vote mattered, which it doesn't, I'd say he is a Hall of Famer.

Greg Maddux, a future Hall of Famer himself, won 15 or more games for the 11th consecutive season in 1998. In 1995, he won his fourth consecutive Cy Young award, and since joining the Braves in 1993 he's dominated National League hitters like precious few before him.

Chapter 3

"He's one of the most focused, concentrated guys I've ever seen."

I didn't know Mark McGwire when I got to Oakland in 1990, but I had heard about him. When we got here in St. Louis . . . let me put it like this: If somebody had bet me 10 years ago that anybody could have hit the ball that far consistently, I'd have lost everything. I'd have lost my house. I mean, I'd have lost everything.

I've seen some big guys hit home runs. I've seen guys hit the ball a long ways. But this guy's consistent and he's stronger than those guys. His skill is what makes him so consistent. That and the fact that he works hard. He really works at what he does. Evidently he's learned a lot along the way, such as how to use his strength and how to use his bat speed. He's got a tremendously short, quick bat.

As a teammate, you know, he's all business. He's one of the most focused, concentrated guys I've ever seen, especially when you consider what he went through in 1998. He does what he has to do, and that's it. He doesn't say much. He jokes a little bit, just like any other man. He's just a good all-around man. And that shows. Everybody sees that every day.

In early September 1998, Major League Baseball began introducing specially marked balls into Cardinals games whenever McGwire was at-bat. To ensure the authenticity of the ball in case of a home run, the first base umpire was instructed to mark the ball with a special pen and put the ball in play only when McGwire was hitting.

And it's not Mac's fault. It's just amazing that one person can generate all this commotion. It's just an awesome, unbelievable situation in the history of this game. You find yourself being more of a fan with all this stuff.

The players appreciate the way he's handled it. He won't talk about himself after the game unless he was a factor. He gives other people their due. To me, Mark is one of the most sincere, humble, real people out there. He can put himself where we are. In other words, he understands what's going on around him.

He doesn't really speak much. I didn't see much of him in Oakland since I was only there for a month and a half in 1990 at the end of the year. When I saw him then, he was always on the trainer's table doing pushups and sit-ups. Then to be around him here in St. Louis, you can see he's a good guy. He's a real professional. He's a good father. He's got a lot of good in him. And he's real about it.

Willie McGee played alongside McGwire when the A's acquired him in a pennant-race trade late in the 1990 season, and again when Big Mac came to St. Louis in 1997. McGee, not a bad hitter himself, won two National League batting championships in his first stint with the Cardinals from 1982 to 1990 and was the NL MVP in 1985.

In the 1993 and '94 seasons, Mark had just 219 combined at-bats. A stress fracture in his left heel as well as back problems slowed Big Mac both seasons.

Chapter 4

"I've ... have been ... and Cardinals ... over the years, and he fits in with all of ... those."

The first time I saw Mark McGwire was last year when we got him, and we were certainly very fortunate to get him. He did a favor for Tony La Russa to come over here, really. And Walt Jocketty (the Cardinals GM) did a great job getting him. But then again, our owners went ahead and signed him for three years, and that was, of course, a good move.

With Mark, you know, every swing is a potential home run. He has power to all fields. He knows the strike zone. He doesn't swing at many bad balls. He gets a lot of walks, and he has a lot of patience. It's good that he's so selective. You can rarely hit bad balls. Not too many bad-ball hitters are really good hitters.

The other thing about him is that he's excited St. Louis fans and he's excited the fans of the country. That Roger Maris thing in 1961 was a New York thing. That was between Maris and Babe Ruth, two Yankees. And hardly any writers ever came to us and asked us about what we thought. But this thing now is not only a St. Louis thing, it's kind of a national thing. It's a good thing for baseball. It's good for fan interest. Fans are talking baseball, thinking baseball, coming out to the games all over the league. He's bringing out more people, you know, which is terrific.

Mark's a great guy. I've had the chance to speak with him a few times, especially down in spring training. He's a truly high-class guy, and a very nice guy. I've never talked about hitting with him. I had such a different hitting style of hitting, you know, my stance, my crouch and all that, so I very seldom talk to anyone about hitting. Ted Williams and I do a lot of talking about hitting, only because he wants to talk about hitting all the time.

But Mark has a natural home run swing, a nice level swing. He has a short swing, but he can hit the ball out of any ballpark. Frank Howard was the biggest guy around in the days when I played. Howard could hit 'em far. He was a big guy, a very powerful guy. But I think the only guy I saw who could hit long home runs like Mark was Mickey Mantle. Yeah, Mantle hit the ball a long

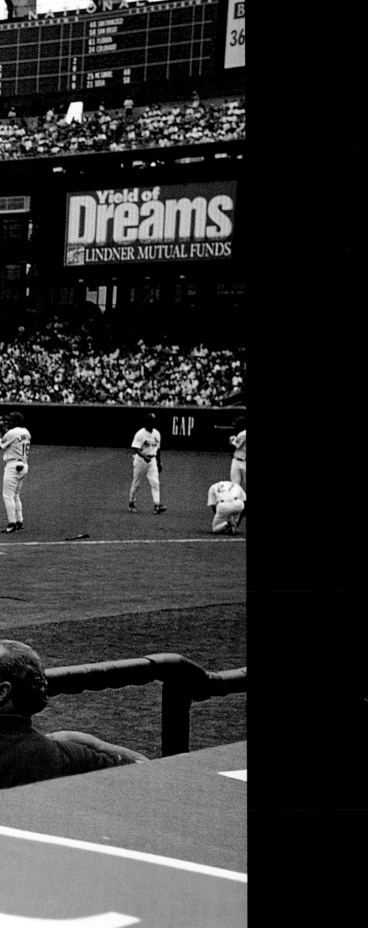

"With Mark, you know, every swing is a potential home run. He has to answer to all the gods."

After playing three years at USC, Mark was drafted 10th overall by the Oakland A's in the 1984 free agent draft.

probably have more fans around the country than any team except maybe the Yankees. They have a great following too. But you go to New York, you run into Cardinals fans. You go to the West Coast, you run into Cardinals fans.

There have been some great Cardinals over the years, and he fits in with all of them. He plays well. He's a good first baseman, too, you know. He's a smart baserunner. He's been around a lot of years and he's a real pro. The Cardinals are on TV now 126 games a year, and my wife, Lil, and I watch Cardinal games all the time. She's a great fan. And if she's not watching when McGwire comes up, I call her in so she can watch him hit.

Stan Musial, Hall of Fame class of 1969, played for the St. Louis Cardinals from 1941-'63. Stan the Man, who now resides in St. Louis, holds the modern National League record for consecutive years (16) hitting .300 or better, was named NL MVP three times, and appeared in a record 24 All-Star games.

Chapter 5

"The obvious thing
that has changed
about him over the
years is his maturity.
Like everyone else,
he grew up."

When you're a rookie, that's the way you think.

We didn't even use aliases when we checked into the team hotel. Both of us were very naive to the major leagues. We'd get our room and we'd be registered as "Mark McGwire" and "Terry Steinbach." We didn't know anything about putting a hold on our phone calls. The phone would ring and we would have to decipher whether it was important enough to answer or not. He was getting a lot of phone calls because of all the home runs. A lot of times the call would be for Mac and he would be sitting there and it was a reporter or someone he didn't know, and I would say, "No, no. Mark's not here right now. He's at the gym lifting weights."

Plus, a lot of it back then was sort of an etiquette thing. You didn't use aliases at that time. If you put down a different name than your own on the rooming list, the veterans would get all over you for it. I remember Don Baylor really would give you grief when he was on

In 1987, Bash Brothers Jose Canseco and Mark McGwire combined for 80 home runs and 231 RBI.

"We wou
both ge
lost tryin
to figure
what doe
to go int
get to th
clubhou

the team in 1988. You would put something down like Willie Nelson and Don would jump you, "Why are you Willie Nelson but I'm just Don Baylor?"

I think Mac has always been into weight-lifting as long as I've known him. He likes to work out. He enjoys that time. He's not into putting 18 heavy plates on the barbell at once to impress people. He just goes in there day after day, very set on what his routine is. He's very specific about what muscle group he's going to be working on. At the end of each season, Mac would say, "I'm going to come in 10 pounds heavier next spring." And I'd say, "Shoot, big deal. So will I. That's just a given." But the difference would be his 10 pounds would be all muscle. He just steadily got a little stronger each year.

Back then, there was a feeling that a baseball player shouldn't lift weights. They thought that you would get all tight and lose flexibility. So we didn't have a strength coach with the Athletics the way teams do now. Dave McKay was one of our coaches, and he had a real big physique and was interested in weight-training. He had a view back then that weight-lifting could be translated into baseball and make you better, and he got a lot of players interested. He would say, "I'm going to the gym at 10 in the morning tomorrow. If you want to join me, come along." A lot of guys did.

Mac and Jose Canseco were the Bash Brothers because we all bashed our arms together after home runs. And did it hurt? Tell me about it. I had to bat behind Mac, so I always had to bash with him at home plate. And he's a big man. A very, very big man. And then he throws in that adrenaline rush from a home run on top of it. Ouch.

He's got 400-plus home runs and they all pretty much run together for me. But distance-wise, the one that really stands out in my mind was in Chicago at the new Comiskey Park a couple of years ago. That one went up on the catwalk. And of course, there was the home run to win the World Series game in 1988. You can't get much bigger than that. Even in Little League or in your backyard playing base-

Mark's first major league hit was against the Yankees' Tommy John on Aug. 24, 1986. His first big-league homer came the next day against Detroit's Walt Terrell.

ball, you dream about that.

When he hits one, it's the presentation that's phenomenal. It's the way players — not the media, not the fans — will come out and watch him take batting practice. But the most noticeable sign that he was something special was this thing we did along with batting practice. We'd do soft-toss, where someone would flip the ball at you from a short distance and you would hit it into this small net that was attached to a weighted support. We'd all hit balls into the net and our hits would maybe pick up the net a little bit. Mac would be the last to hit, and when he took his swings, the ball would go into the net so hard that the thing would rise off the ground. We'd be standing around watching him and saying, "What's wrong with the rest of us?" But it was a good thing to teach us to stay within ourselves as players. We knew we couldn't do what he could do, so we didn't even try.

He's a very smart hitter. He's intelligent up there. He doesn't just have tremendous bat speed. He doesn't just swing the bat as hard as he can every time. He's also a very smart hitter and has a very good eye and puts a lot of work into it.

McGwire spent the 1985 season with Class A Modesto as the starting third baseman. He hit .274, with 24 homers and 50 extrabase hits in 138 games, earning him California League Rookie of the Year honors.

The obvious thing that has changed about him over the years is his maturity. Like everyone else, he grew up. That's just a natural thing. There's no secret about that. Experience, time in the game, age . . . it all matures you. If you ask me if he's more outgoing now than he was his rookie year, I'd say no. But he is more experienced. He's more experienced with doing interviews, so he knows how to say things better. He's probably done hundreds of interviews; no, thousands of them.

Like I said, I didn't look at him then the way he was is now. Back then, he was a roommate. He was a teammate. He was a good friend.

And he still is.

Terry Steinbach broke into the big leagues with Mark McGwire in 1987. The catcher went on to make the American League All-Star team three times, including 1988 when he was the game's MVP, before joining the Minnesota Twins in 1997 so he could finish his career in his home state.

Chapter 6

'You're looking in the neighborhood of 8,000 home runs that Mark McGwire has hit off me over 10 years."

Mark McGwire's a good friend of mine. We've been together for a lot years. I met him when he first came up to the majors in 1986. We had heard that he broke all the home run records at USC, so we knew we had a power hitter. That's what we signed. But he was a big third baseman in the minor leagues.

My first impression when I watched him take batting practice was that he certainly had a lot of power. It was interesting to see how he matched up with Jose Canseco, who we already had. And they were right there with each other. Each day, it was a duel to see which one would hit the ball the farthest. They were both big-swing guys, which can be a bad thing, too. It probably worked more against Jose than it did McGwire. Jose had a nice stroke where he used the whole field. If he concentrated on more of that, he probably would have hit .340, .350. But maybe that's not fair. You always expect more out of somebody.

The point I make with people here about McGwire is that when I throw to him, he's not just putting on a show. In batting practice, he does what he does in the games. He gets up on the plate, and what he basically does is pull the ball and hit the ball in the air. He does not hit ground balls. He does not hit into double plays.

Since he's doing in batting practice exactly what he does in a game, it doesn't hurt his swing. Some guys want to come out in batting practice and try to impress the fans and hit it deep when their game is more suited to using the whole field. Like Jose Canseco. And Ken Griffey Jr.'s another one. Just guessing, but that's probably a big reason why Griffey didn't

does he hit a ball off the screen right in front of me. And he doesn't hit a whole lot of line drives. A lot of pitchers can be thankful for that, because if he became a line-drive hitter and started hitting balls up the middle, I'd start worrying for some pitchers. But in batting practice, I know that screen's there. I use every bit of it, just in case. And he'll hit it every now and then.

I don't worry about everybody watching me. I'm confident throwing the ball over the plate. I don't feed it on the inside corner so he can pull it farther, like people may think I do. I throw the ball more over the middle. Throwing inside doesn't help him. That's the last pitch he's going to see in a game. But if I pitched him they way they do in the games, I probably wouldn't throw him any strikes. You throw him middle, middle. And if the ball happens to move on the outside part of the plate, fine. And if it happens to come inside, fine. He's real comfortable with me.

We've done it for so long, there's a little rhythm he and I get into. It's a little rhythm where you take more time with your pitches to him. Most coaches like to get into a rhythm where they throw, step back, pick up a ball, throw, step back, pick up a ball, and they don't like to be stopped. If someone else comes up there, I'll just start throwing, Boom! Boom! Boom! But Mark concentrates more than any kid I've ever seen.

If you watch him take batting practice, he looks down at his feet, he looks at his bat, he gets his little thing going, and then he comes back with the bat ready to go. I see him doing his thing, then I move and here I come. It's a little rhythm where he takes a little time, just like he does when he's up in a game. It takes a little more time, but that's the way he likes it, and that's what we do.

We jokingly talked about taking me to Denver for the home run contest at the All-Star Game. But we were just joking. I wouldn't have done that. It would be demeaning to me and embarrassing to Mark. I would much rather spend my three days for the All-Star break in Scottsdale, Ariz., with my wife rather than going out there and throwing batting practice at the All-Star Game.

I've been asked about being Mark's personal batting practice pitcher, which is kind of insulting, really. I'm the outfield coach. I'm also the baserunning coach. I coach first base. Just one of the things I do as a coach is to throw batting practice. Every team has a coach doing the throwing. It doesn't bother me, really, but when I hear it I do remind them that I do other things.

Now let's see . . . Mark and I were together for about eight years together in Oakland. Then he came here last year, so that's about 10 years together. And there are 162 games in a year. We take batting practice, a conservative figure, about 100 times a year. And he'll probably hit eight or 10 homers, conservatively, every time. Let's say he averages eight. So that's 800 a year, conservatively. You're looking in the neigh-

borhood of 8,000 home runs that Mark McGwire has hit off me over 10 years. Then somebody said, "Hey, what about spring training?" So there's another 2,000. That's a lot of home runs. That's a lot to choose from.

But I really don't see too many of them. I don't have time to watch, actually, because there are other guys in that group and they want their time to hit. If I'm standing there watching Mark's homers, the other guys are going to get half the swings. But when I know he really caught one, I'll put a little stall on, and look back to see where it goes.

There are certain ballparks that have structures where you can see the distance of a ball. An example would be out in Phoenix, where I'm from. When we played the Diamondbacks, I hadn't seen the inside of the stadium until we played there. I woke up that morning reading about these windows that they can open out in the outfield, and people were wondering if Mark could actually hit one through one of those big windows. That would be a ball that actually would be hit right out of the stadium. But the windows are way, way out there.

So when I got down there, the first thing I looked for were these windows. And about the third pitch he hit, he hit it real good. And I turned around and took a peek, and it hit right off the middle of one window. It wasn't open. I actually started laughing when he did that. They did that little skit at the All-Star Game about somebody driving his car out of the parking lot because McGwire might be taking batting practice. Well, he hit one off me once in Denver that actually did that. The ball went over the left side of the scoreboard there and down into the parking lot.

As Mark approached No. 62, his batting practice home run balls were selling for as much as $1,000.

That's where all that started. They talk about that one. Those are two of the longest ones. But he's gone to center field here at Busch Stadium. That one to center field, where they put a Band-Aid where it hit on the Post-Dispatch sign, that's a poke way up there. And he's gone to left field upper deck here, and that's a serious poke.

The thing about batting practice is, he doesn't want to turn it into a sideshow. But you know what's fun about it — and Mark sees it this way, too — is the fans having fun with it. Fans are actually coming out early and loading up in the seats and watching this show. And the nice part about it is, we're not putting on a show to do it. Mark's just doing what he does. We went to Colorado, and they said, "The Barnum & Bailey Circus is coming to town. Come on out and see Mark McGwire take batting practice." I didn't like to hear them refer to it like that. Mark couldn't care less how far they go out.

I know if I wasn't there, they'd just get somebody else to throw to him. But we've been doing this a long time. I know we get wrapped up in it sometimes. Sometimes he lines a ball up the middle, lines another one up the middle, and then maybe hits a line drive to left. And I'll say to myself, "Okay, the people want to see him hit it far." And I'll throw one a little inside, and he hits one way up there, and everybody's roaring again. So you have a tendency every now and then to slip one in there and let him go ahead and crush it.

Dave McKay was in his third season as the Cardinals' first base coach when Mark McGwire broke Roger Maris' record. McKay coached in Oakland from 1984-1995 after an eight-year playing career with the Twins, Blue Jays and A's in the late '70s and early '80s.

Chapter 7

"He has a quick swing. The bat head comes through the hitting area with great velocity."

On Saturday, Sept. 12, Randy Johnson walked McGwire, giving Big Mac an NL-record 152 free passes, at the time still 18 short of Babe Ruth's major league record set in 1923.

"He's a patient hitter up there. He's particular about what balls he's gonna swing at."

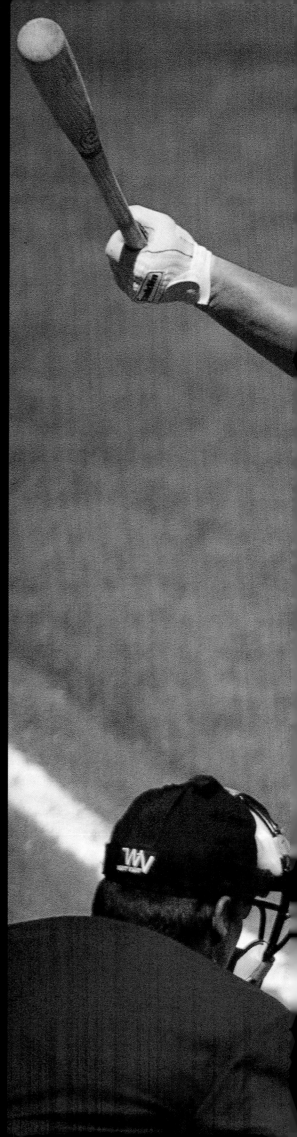

to right-center field. He had that kind of power then.

And he was using the wooden bat then, not the aluminum. I saw then how the ball jumped off his bat. That's what you get when you have a nice easy swing, you're strong and you make solid contact. He has a quick swing. The bat head comes through the hitting area with great velocity. And he always had that short swing. The shorter your stroke, the quicker you get to the ball.

Sammy Sosa's doing the same thing. The thing about Sammy is, he idolized that other guy who played right field and wore No. 21, Roberto Clemente. In Pittsburgh, when Sammy hit his 57th and 58th home runs, there was kind of a shadow out there in right field. Sammy probably was thinking he was going to perform well for Roberto, like the guy was looking down to see if Sammy was doing a good job. Sammy often talked about Clemente when he first came to the big leagues, and Sammy knows I played against Clemente. So he's asked a lot of questions about Clemente, and I've gotten Sammy tapes (of Clemente playing).

It took Mark 144 games and Sammy Sosa 150 to reach 61 home runs. Maris reached 61 in 163 games, and Ruth hit 60 in 154.

A lot of power hitters who played with me weren't as big as Mark. Clemente weighed 185. Willie Mays was about 185 pounds. Ernie Banks was about 178. Lou Brock weighed 175, 178. My swing was short and quick when I was playing. It had to be. We weren't big, but we were strong. The biggest guy when I played, I guess, was Willie Stargell. He was a pretty big guy. And then Willie McCovey. But the guys now, they're big, strong and quick. They do a lot of weight-lifting, like McGwire. When I played with the Cubs, we had that thing called an exergenie in the clubhouse. We pulled on it and did exercises with it for about a week. Then a couple of pitchers got sore arms, and Leo Durocher, the manager, threw all that stuff out of there. He told the clubhouse guy, "Get this stuff out of here. I don't want to see it again."

So we didn't get into lifting weights and doing all that extra stuff. You also have to consider the fact that we had to work in the off-season, because we didn't make the money they do now. The players today, and I don't blame 'em, they play baseball. And after the season, they stay on vacation maybe

two weeks, or three weeks, and they get right back in the gym. Most of these fellows when they go to spring training, all they have to do is get in baseball shape.

When we went to spring training, we had to lose weight, some of that little extra weight that some of the guys pick up, like pitchers. And then we got in baseball shape because we didn't do anything in the off-season but work, eat, sleep, and drink beer.

When I see McGwire hit now, he looks like the same guy I saw in '84, except bigger. He's put on a lot of weight. I tell him every time I see him, "It seems like you get bigger and bigger." He just laughs.

And there's another thing a lot of people don't look at. Mark went over there to St. Louis last year from Oakland, and he got back into a comfortable situation. He had all those guys from Oakland with him. He had Tony La Russa, the manager. He had the coaching staff. The trainer is there now. Walt Jocketty was an aide to Alderson, and he's the general manager in St. Louis. When Mark got there, they had some guys he played with on the A's,

Mark McGwire was originally drafted by the Montreal Expos out of Damien High School (Claremont, Calif.) in the eighth round of the June 1981 free agent draft, but he elected instead to play college baseball at the University of Southern California.

the next one three or four inches outside. And that's the way they keep drawing you outside to hit the ball. The thing you should do as a hitter when you come up to the big leagues is, you start taking pitches. And then you get the umpires on your side.

I never did ask an umpire, "Was that a strike or was that a ball?" You ask him that, and he'll think, "This guy doesn't know what a strike or a ball is." I know what's a strike or a ball. I don't have to ask the umpire. And when you start doing that, they know a lot of times that when you take pitches, they don't have to be strikes.

When I came up, I established a good rapport with the umpires. And there are times you can get the call on a pitch that's close. But you can't swing at a ball way up high, and the next pitch you let one go and say, "That wasn't a strike." The umpire'll say, "How do you know? You swung at that last pitch over your head."

The umpires don't give Mark anything. He earned it by having a good eye. Ted Williams had that kind of eye. Carl Yazstremski had that eye. Mark Grace on our team has that kind of eye. People know that Mark Grace is a good ball-strike hitter. Same with McGwire. And umpires know this. They might look at a pitch a little closer, because they know he has a pretty good eye. And he knows where the strike zone is.

Billy Williams, Hall of Fame class of 1987, left Oakland to coach in Chicago in 1985, just before Mark McGwire made himself a permanent fixture at first base for the A's. During his 18-year career (1959-1976), 16 seasons of which with the Cubs, Williams hit 426 homers.

Chapter 8

"What the home
run race is doing
is bringing back
the star system
to baseball."

"People can identify with guys like Mark McGwire, Ken Griffey Jr. and Sammy Sosa."

So when I saw him in the spring of 1998, I said, "Here's a pretty good hitter. He's not just a slugger." I don't know who put that label on him. But when you hit 49 homers your first year, they're going to put that "slugger" label on you. He's fundamentally sound, let me put it that way. Even running the bases. He is a good baserunner. He gets the mileage out of what he has. He's not a speedster, but he

The guy who caught home run No. 63 off the bat of Mark McGwire told the Cardinals organization he would return the ball if they met more than 30 of his demands. Included in the list was a trip to spring training, items autographed by McGwire and Stan Musial, and the chance for the guy and his son to throw out first pitches at Cardinals games. The organization respectfully declined the offer.

doesn't just run from one base to the other one. I saw one game where the outfielder bobbled the ball and had Mark not been running full speed, he wouldn't have taken the extra base. That tells me he's not a station-to-station runner, that he's always looking at the ball, and that he's ready to see that

moment and go on to the extra base. That's what impresses me: heads-up baseball.

The home run chase was exciting for baseball. In his case, when he hits home runs, it's not just another home run. He hits extraordinary home runs. That's what sets him apart.

One of the highlights of Mark's career came in the 1988 World Series when his solo homer in Game 3 off the Dodgers' Jay Howell in the bottom of the ninth inning gave Oakland a 2-1 win.

What the home run race is doing is bringing back the star system to baseball, or at the least highlighting the need for the star system. People can identify with guys like Mark McGwire, Ken Griffey Jr. and Sammy Sosa. People don't say, "Who do these guys play for?" That's a good example of the star system. Look at Michael Jordan in pro basketball. The NBA had a team system for years and they couldn't sell tickets. Then they went to the star system and sold everything out. With baseball, people have said, "Where have the DiMaggios and Musials gone?" People quit watching baseball and went over to basketball.

Until the mid-'90s, the star system was always around in baseball. It started with Babe Ruth, but they did have guys like Ty Cobb prior to that. The whole thing was based on the star system. But it was tough in the mid-'90s with the free agents and the players going from team to team. Players don't get a chance to establish themselves. But Mark McGwire's proving that you can do it with another team.

But it does illustrate, again, that the star system is a fundamentally a sound system. If the team loses, people still have a reason to come to the ballpark. But if you're on the team system and you're 18 to 20 games out late in the season, nobody comes to the games.

What I like about McGwire is that he goes around and does his job and he plays the game hard. When he hits a home run, it's what I call the 20-second syndrome. It used to take us about 20 seconds to go around the bases on a home run. Now it takes some guys a week to go around the bases. When I played, if a guy took that much time, the next time up they decked him. I don't think anybody ever tried decking McGwire, but if they did, that'd probably just make him mad. And then you don't know what would happen. Then he probably WOULD hit one far.

I do, however, think my National League stolen base record is safe from him. But you never know. He may turn it on.

Lou Brock, Hall of Fame class of 1985, was just the 14th player to amass 3,000 hits. His 938 stolen bases are still a National League record, and he also holds the record for career batting average in the World Series with a .391 average in 20 games.

Chapter 9

"Mark is very, very particular about his bats. He's used the same model forever."

STADIUM EXTRA

TUESDAY, SEPTEMBER 8, 1998

50¢

62 UNBELIEVABLE CLASS

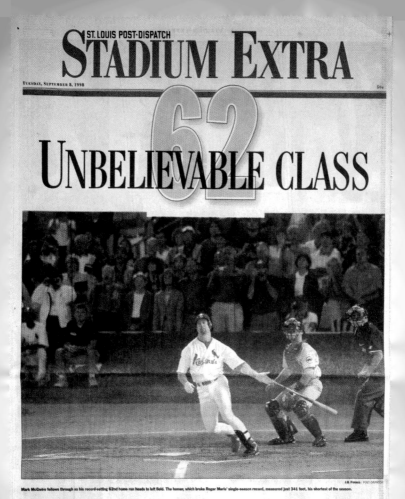

Mark McGwire follows through as his record-setting 62nd home run heads to left field. The homer, which broke Roger Maris' single-season record, measured just 341 feet, his shortest of the season.

J.B. FORBES / POST-DISPATCH

McGwire hails St. Louis as he stands alone with the single-season home run record

BY TOM TIMMERMANN
Of the Post-Dispatch

With a blast that rocked both Busch Stadium and the baseball world, the Cardinals' Mark McGwire hit his 62nd home run of the season Tuesday night, breaking Roger Maris' single-season home run record, a mark that for years had looked unbreakable.

McGwire slammed the first pitch from Chicago righthander Steve Trachsel just over the wall in left field at Busch Stadium with two outs and no one on in the fourth inning. McGwire jumped into the arms of first base coach Dave McKay, almost missing first in the process. He received congratulations from every member of the Cubs as he rounded the bases.

After touching home plate, McGwire lifted and hugged his son, Matthew, as he was joined by teammates, who poured on to the field. As fireworks went off overhead, McGwire received a standing ovation that lasted 10 minutes.

McGwire climbed into the stands to talk with Maris' family, who had come to St. Louis for the historic event. Cubs rightfielder Sammy Sosa, who came into the game with 58 homers, came in to congratulate McGwire as well.

McGwire addressed the crowd after the homer, thanking St. Louis, his teammates and opponents, especially Sosa, for their "unbelievable class."

McGwire tied Maris' single-season home run record by hitting No. 61 on Monday in the first inning off Cubs pitcher Mike Morgan. That home run bounced off the Stadium Club windows in left field before dropping into the left-field stands.

McGwire's 62nd homer was an amazing exclamation point on one of the most incredible performances in baseball history. He already had broken or tied dozens of other records over the course of the season, including becoming the first player ever to hit 50 or more homers in three successive seasons.

But of all the records he has set, none stands as large as the single-season home run record. The mark has been held by just two players — Maris and Babe Ruth — since Ruth first claimed the record in 1919 and the numbers 60 and 61 have stood for years as seemingly unreachable standards.

Almost as amazing is the speed with which McGwire reached the record. He hit his 61st in the Cardinals' 144th game. Maris hit his 61st homer in the Yankees' 163rd game.

Walt Jocketty (Cardinals general manager) came to me in 1997 and said, "We're finishing up a deal to acquire Mark McGwire and it looks like it's going to go." Now, this was a week before he joined us in Philadelphia, so I had time to call around and make sure we had "Mark McGwire" Adirondack bats and "Mark McGwire" uniforms and all the particular little needs he would have. So when he met us in Philadelphia, we had everything he needed. He was ready. And he was pretty impressed with that.

As far as the uniform goes, he's got a 35-inch waist and a 52 1/2-inch chest. He's a big man, at 6-5 and 250 pounds. We have to get them specially made. I would say it would take at least two Ozzie Smith shirts to make one Mark McGwire shirt. Ozzie wore a 40. Probably 50 percent of the players in that locker room are

Every one of McGwire's major league homers was hit with a Rawlings Adirondack bat.

in size 46 shirts.

His first day, though, he still had his Rawlings Adirondack bats from Oakland with the green strip of tape around them. His bats with the red stripe for the Cardinals were not in yet. So we forged his old bats up a little bit, and his regular bats arrived the second day. Normally they come from the factory like that, with the tape. That's how you recognize those Adirondack bats. They come in the color of each team.

He uses a 35/33 bat. That's a 35-inch, 33-ounce bat. That's on the heavy side. Most players use a 31-ounce bat. Although Mark's is not extremely large, it's certainly bigger than normal. We have one or two guys who have 33-ounce bats. Ron Gant uses a 33-ounce, but that's another strong man. Players in general have gone to lighter bats. I guess they feel they can generate more bat speed with a lighter bat.

Mark is very, very particular about his bats. He's used the same model forever. It's real stressful to order bats for him, because if they're not just right when they come in, he's out here in a flash saying, "These aren't right." I hold my breath whenever his bats come in. If they're a quarter of an ounce off, he knows it. He doesn't weight them, but he knows.

Willie McGee is like that as well. His bats came in once and Willie said, "Buddy, these aren't right." I said, "Willie, they say 31 ounce." Willie said, "These are not 31 ounce." So I weighed them, and they were like 30.2 ounces.

McGwire's like that. He'll say, "The head of these bats is not right. It's just not right." And he'll go measure them and come back and say, "Yeah, they're a half inch off" or "They're a quarter inch off." It's amazing how those guys can tell that.

Chapter 10

"I looked back and I saw my brother, but he's not as fast as I am. I knew that if I didn't get the ball, he'd get it."

There were four or five other guys from the grounds crew with me just behind the left field wall. One of them was my brother, Tino. I was standing on this platform that lets you see over the top of the fence.

It was McGwire's second at-bat of the day. I wasn't thinking anything different than what I normally think when he bats. All season I'd watched him hit home runs over my head, and I just wanted to see No. 62. I wanted to be there for it. Once I heard the crack of the bat, I saw the ball was hit so low and so hard, and I thought, "You know, that might have a chance to fit between the wall and the bottom of the second level." As the ball was sailing through the air, I thought: "A, it's going to hit the wall; or B, a fan's going to get it." Then, I thought, "Man, this might go through!"

So I jumped down on this big sandbag below the wall — it's almost like a big beanbag — and I started running. I think it shocked my brother and all these guys initially. They weren't sure what was really going on. And as I scampered away, I could see the ball had hit off the net that's used for the batting cage out there and had just dropped right there. As I ran, I looked back one time and saw my brother, but he's not as fast as I am. He had a big smile. I knew that if I didn't get the ball,

When he hit his 62nd home run, the only count on which McGwire had not homered was 3-0.

he'd get it. But I picked up the ball and my hands went completely numb. I shoved it in my pocket. All the guys were going crazy, and I was going crazy.

We started running toward the tunnel that goes to the clubhouse. We got about halfway there before I remembered "Operation 62." After McGwire hit No. 62, we were supposed be out on the field — not only to make sure a spectator didn't run out on the field, but to pick up all the streamers and confetti after the celebration. So I turned around and yelled, "We've got Operation 62!" The ball was still in my right pocket, and we all ran back out on the field. My brother was right by my side. And as we were picking up the streamers, I looked at him and said, "What do I do?" Meaning, where do I go from here? I knew I was going to give the ball back. I just didn't know how to do it.

So I just kept picking up more streamers and confetti. And once the field was cleared, I thought the best and quickest way was to go through that tunnel. So I ran back through underneath the stands. I saw an usher, Richard, at the visiting clubhouse and I said, "Richard, I've got the ball." He couldn't believe it.

Just past there is the Cardinal Club, where my mother works. I just smoked it through there. Didn't stop to tell her. I ran down into the Cardinal clubhouse, but I really didn't know what to do there. Nobody was there. Obviously, they were all out celebrating. I was going to leave it in McGwire's locker, but I thought, "Naw, I think this ball's a little too valuable to do that."

I ran back down into the actual dugout, and the first person I saw there was Steve Peeler, my boss on the grounds

Then I had like a whirlwind tour. I went to Disney World, and they treated me better probably than Mickey Mouse. My family and Steve, my boss, went, too. I owe Steve that, because he's the one who hired me and let me come back (to work) after I went to Chicago to train for Anderson Marketing. While I was at the Magic Kingdom, I did all these TV interviews. I did the "Today" show, "Good Morning America," the CBS morning show, CNN and MSNBC.

While I was in Orlando, I got to meet President Clinton. He looked real tired. It was a real honor, though. He thanked me for giving the ball back. And we talked about how baseball had gone from having some problems during the strike years to being on a pinnacle, really. It was really funny, then, because Steve invited him to a game. And he said he'd see what he could do about actually coming.

Steve said he thinks 99 out of 100 people support me for giving the ball back, but I really think it's 100 percent. Well, I know a few people have written that I should have sold the ball to take care of my family, when I get one. Now that I've had a few days to think about it, I think it's such a personal decision. I just hope that nobody criticizes me or the gentleman in Chicago who got Sammy Sosa's 62nd home run ball. If another person sold the ball, I'd respect that decision.

People have been writing and thanking me that they can now go and see the ball at the Hall of Fame. It's been wild. A writer somewhere out on the West Coast wrote that since I gave up a million-dollar ball, people should send me a dollar to make up for it. I've been getting letters with dollar bills and $5 bills and even a $20 check. One gentleman just wrote, "Bravo," and put $2 in with a copy of the article. That just shows how great America is. But I'm not keeping the money. Whatever I get, I split between Cardinal Care, the team's charity, and Mr. McGwire's foundation for abused children.

I wonder if it was destiny for me to get the ball. I knew exactly what I wanted to do with it. And now it's up to everybody else to do what's right. If they want to give a dollar to Cardinal Care or Mr. McGwire's foundation, that's great.

I just know that what I did, I did it because I felt it was the right thing to do.

Tim Forneris, 22, from Collinsville, Ill., has been a part-time Cardinals groundskeeper for two years. A graduate of St. Louis University, he finished a company training course in Chicago a week before rejoining the grounds crew and becoming a part of baseball history.

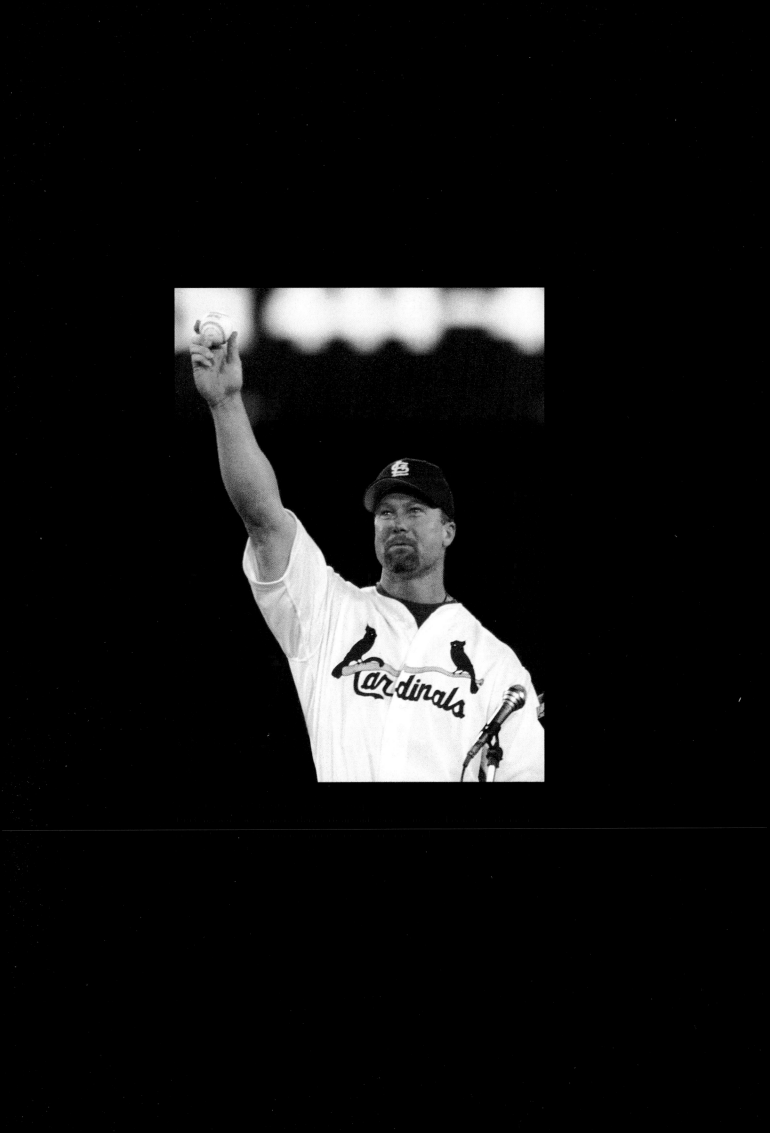

Chapter 11

"There are millions of kids waking up in the morning now, asking their parents if Sosa or McGwire hit one last night."

For Mark McGwire this is an affirmation of what a huge portion of his career has been about. He is the all-time leader now in home runs per at-bats. Even if he did not hit 60 home runs this year, if he never threatened the record, he would still be part of any knowledgeable discussion of the greatest home run hitters of all time.

If you confined the argument only to five or six players, he'd have to be in that discussion. So his breaking the record or threatening the record is an extension of what he's already established. That's why the focus is legitimately on him. That and the fact that his blasts are absolutely Ruthian, and he's a Bunyanesque-looking guy.

He also gets a lot of attention because he got out of the box first. If Sammy Sosa had his 20-home run month in April or May (instead of June), there'd be a different sense of the race. But McGwire foreshadowed it last year with a 58-homer season. And not just with the 58, but with the rush that he closed with (15 HRs in September). So, he's done it for most of his career. Then this season he set the pace early. Then throw in the 500-footers and the batting practice home runs, and the stage was set.

Now had Ken Griffey Jr. been with McGwire homer for homer at the outset, I think the attention on both of them would have been equal. Griffey's already established. Coming into this season, he probably passed Barry Bonds in the public perception as the game's best player. But he fell off the pace. And Sammy Sosa stepped up his pace. Everyone loves Sammy Sosa. He's a happy guy who exudes cheerfulness and has an inspiring rags-to-riches background. The rest of his career may

(NEWS foto by Frank Hurley)
Maris swings and baseball goes. Some 360 feet away, it dropped into the right field stands and Roger had become first man ever to hit 61 homers in season.

Yogi Berra (8) and batboy are the first to congratulate Ma

One for the Books

(NEWS foto by Bob Olen)

has just delivered ball and Roger blasted. Arrow shows ball's trajectory into record book.

Right field stand is a forest of upstretched arms as Sal Durante, a 19-year-old truck driver from Coney Island, reaches highest and makes one-handed catch (arrow). The grab will be worth $5,000 to Durante, that sum being promised by a California businessman for returning the ball to Maris.

(NEWS foto by Frank Hurley)

(NEWS foto by Jim Mooney)

rank Hurley)

Roger holds Yankee uniform 61 after his historic feat. Maris blasted the record-breaker in his 163d and last game of the season. Babe Ruth established the record of 60 in 155 games in 1927.

Stories on pages 3 and 52; other pictures page one and back page

(NEWS foto by Jim Mooney)

Jubilant Sal Durante holds ball. Girl friend Rosemarie Calabrese is with him.

prove that this was the beginning of a run of several years at this level, or something close to it. But that's a big question.

If McGwire does it, people will say, "That's the guy. He deserves to do it. He's been at this level for awhile now." And even this year, as great as what Sosa and Griffey are doing, their home runs per at-bats aren't even close to what McGwire has (one HR per 7.7 at-bats as of early September). For that matter, McGwire's home runs per at-bats are much better than Babe Ruth in '27 (1:9) or Roger Maris in '61 (1:9.67).

For one year, Roger Maris was worthy. The reason why more people rooted for Mickey Mantle wasn't just that he was the established and more popular guy in New York, which he was. More importantly, Mickey Mantle was already in the discussion with the greatest players in baseball history. The home run chase was an extension of his career. With Maris, it really is an anomaly. He was a fine all-around player, but never approached that performance in any other season. Mantle hit 52 homers when he won the Triple Crown in '56. He hit more home runs per time at-bat than Maris did in '61. Mantle hit 54 homers in 514 at-bats (1:9.52). Maris hit 61 in 590.

Ruth had invented the home run. He led the league with 11 in 1918. Then he led the league the next year with 29, which was the record. The two records he held, appropriately — the single-season and career home run records — were symbols of the larger truth. Which is that he was baseball's all-time greatest power hitter. He was synonymous with the home run. He was the Sultan of Swat. So it was right that he hold those records.

Look at it this way. Everyone who hit 50 home runs prior to Roger Maris has been inducted into the Hall of Fame. Hack Wilson. Jimmie Foxx. Hank Greenberg. Ralph Kiner won seven home run titles in 10 years and hit 50 twice. Johnny Mize. Mantle and Mays each would hit 50 twice. And of course Ruth, who did it four times. So any of those guys who even approached Ruth's record were Hall of Famers.

Then along comes Maris. He had been the MVP the year before, but he never hit .300 in his career. So that caused people to have mixed feelings about him. I think there's much as an

Mark still holds the Pac 10 Conference record for homers in a season with 32. He was The Sporting News' 1984 College Player of the Y...

the overall interest in baseball has gone up.

Nothing against Mark McGwire or Sammy Sosa, but in the last two years, the team record of 240 home runs that the Yankees set — which stood since 1961 — has been broken in consecutive years. The Orioles broke it in '96 and Seattle broke Baltimore's record in '97. There were a half-dozen guys with a shot at 50 home runs this year. In the first three decades after Maris hit 61, only three guys (Mays, George Foster and Cecil Fielder) topped 50 — three in 30-

been a great hitter? Yes. But how is it that all these guys hit .400 in the early 1900s and into the 1920s, and no one has hit .400 since 1941?

Conditions change. None of this stuff happens in a vacuum. Could Mark McGwire or Sammy Sosa have broken Roger Maris' record in '68? I don't think so. The numbers that you observe, the way the ball jumps off the bat, all the conditions now favor hitters in general and power hitters in particular. You've got all these guys — even leaving the question of supplements aside — all

Big Mac's 63rd home
run was the 450th of
his career. Just 20
players have hit more,
and just 15 have more
than 500. At age 34,
McGwire seems a sure
bet to reach 500, with
an outside shot at
becoming the fourth

pumped up on weight training. That's something that past generations of ballplayers didn't do. They're swinging lighter bats, therefore at greater speed. And they're swinging at a possibly juiced up baseball — although that's the part that's least convincing to me. Maybe it is juiced up. I don't know.

But the other stuff, I know for sure. Today's power hitters care even less how many times they strike out than a generation ago. You've got a smaller strike zone. Pitching has been diluted through expansion. Most ballparks have homer-friendly dimensions, although in McGwire's case, it should be said that he hits them so far, what difference does it make? They're out of any ballpark.

So what you've got in McGwire and Griffey — and possibly Sosa — are Hall of Fame players who would be great in any era. And they're lucky enough to come along in an era that maximizes what they do especially well. Just like the Deadball Era maximized what Ty Cobb did especially well. Would Ty Cobb have made the Hall of Fame no matter when he played? Of course. Would he win batting titles no matter when he played? Of course.

Would he have won nine straight batting titles in the 1970s and 1980s? And 12 titles in 13 years? And have a lifetime batting average of .367? I don't think so. Not because he was one bit less good, but because the conditions were different.

One last thing: It feels right that the record is being pursued by a Cardinal and a Cub. Great baseball cities. Appreciative fans. Classic settings. It just feels right.

NBC broadcaster Bob Costas discussed Mark McGwire and the significance of the great home run race of '98 from the friendly confines of his office in St. Louis.

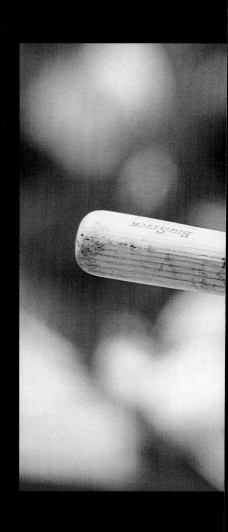

Writers   **Photographers**